THE ART OF BEING LAZY

Small Efforts, Big Impacts

Embracing Simplicity for a More
Joyful and Productive Life.

Inspired By JAMES CLEAR Atomic Habits

JAMES FERRIS

This book is published by Therapy Seminary Publishers.

Paperback Book Edition: ISBN: 978-1963674040

First Edition: 2024

Table of Contents

Dedication

To my beloved parents, whose memories continue to inspire serenity and strength in every word I write. Your spirits live on in the peaceful embrace of this journey.

Introduction

"Ever wondered if the secret to your biggest dreams could be doing... less?"

In a world that glorifies the grind, where being perpetually busy is worn like a badge of honor, "The Art of Laziness" might sound like a paradoxical fantasy. But what if I told you that this book holds the key to unlocking a life where success doesn't come from running yourself ragged, but from strategic inactivity?

Right now, you're standing at the crossroads of a life-altering choice. Close this book, and you might forever wonder if you could have had a life of achievement without the endless hustle. Keep reading, and you'll step into a world where 'laziness' is the unexpected hero, the hidden genius behind a fulfilled and balanced life.

Imagine, for a moment, a life where stress is a choice, not a given. A life where productivity doesn't drain you but energizes you. This isn't a far-fetched dream; it's the reality waiting for you in these pages.

Let me paint you a picture. There was once a person, much like you, who believed that success equated to constant motion, to never hitting the pause button. Yet, they felt like a hamster on a wheel — moving but going nowhere. Then, they dared to embrace 'productive laziness.' The transformation was nothing short of miraculous. They achieved more, not through relentless toil, but through mindful rest. This story isn't a fairy tale. It's a blueprint that you, too, can follow.

In this book, you'll discover the art of making peace with doing less — and in that peace, finding a path to doing what truly matters. You'll learn to break free from the illusion that busyness equals productivity. You'll understand how the power of 'No' can open doors to unforeseen opportunities. You'll redefine what it means to be productive — not as a tireless worker bee, but as a master strategist of your own life.

You'll be introduced to techniques that seem so simple, yet so revolutionary. The 20 Life-Changing Lazy Habits, the Magic of 80/20, and the wisdom of Parkinson's Law applied to everyday life — these are just glimpses of the transformative journey you're about to embark on.

So, I challenge you: Dare to be 'lazy.' Dare to be different. Dare to discover how doing less can surprisingly lead to achieving more.

If you're still here, still reading, there's a part of you that's curious, that's hungry for a change. Trust that instinct. This isn't just another self-help book; it's a manifesto for a new way of living.

Don't just read this book; let it read into you, challenge you, change you. Because on the other side of these pages lies a life where you're not just surviving, but thriving — all through the art of embracing the power of laziness.

Welcome to a journey that defies everything you've been told about success. Welcome to "The Art of Laziness."

PREFACE

Dare to Open?
A playful nudge to start the journey

Are you brave enough to question everything you've been told about hard work?"

This isn't just a chapter. It's an invitation to a journey that might just turn everything you know about success on its head. Dare to Open? It sounds playful, almost like a challenge. But it's more than that. It's a question of whether you're ready to embrace a truth that might be opposite to what you've always believed.

Right now, you're holding a choice in your hands. Turn this page, and you step into a world that challenges the glorification of 'busyness,' where success isn't measured by how exhausted you are at the end of the day. Close the book, and you might remain in the comfortable but limiting embrace of conventional wisdom.

I understand the hesitation. We've been conditioned to think that non-stop working is the only path to achievement. But what if I told you that the key to unlocking your full potential is not more work, but smarter work? This chapter is about breaking free from the chains of the hustle culture. It's about discovering that the most productive days of your life might be the ones where you do the least.

Think about it. How many times have you felt like you're just going through the motions, busy but not productive? It's a cycle that leaves you drained, unfulfilled, and no closer to your goals. It's time to ask yourself: Is this relentless pursuit of 'doing' really bringing me closer to my dreams, or is it just an endless chase?

In the pages that follow, you'll encounter stories, strategies, and insights that will challenge you, inspire you, and maybe even provoke you. You'll learn why some of the most successful people in history were masters of 'productive laziness.' You'll discover how embracing periods of rest and reflection can lead to breakthroughs and innovation.

So, I ask you again: Dare to Open? Are you ready to explore the art of achieving more by doing less? To discover a life where your worth isn't tied to your workload but to your ability to make smart, strategic decisions about your time and energy?

If there's a voice inside you whispering, "Yes," then turn this page. Embrace the curiosity, the skepticism, and the hope that brought you here. Let's embark on this journey together.

Welcome to a new understanding of productivity. Welcome to a life where you dare to open doors you didn't even know existed. Welcome to the transformative power of 'productive laziness'.

PART 1

MASTERING EFFICIENCY AND SUCCESS WITH MINIMAL EFFORT

CHAPTER 1

The Lazy Brilliance

*"Laziness may appear attractive, but work gives satisfaction." - **Anne Frank***

At first glance, Anne Frank's words might seem to contradict the very essence of this book. However, delve deeper, and you'll discover that they highlight a profound truth: work satisfaction isn't about relentless labor; it's about finding the hidden genius in what many hastily label as 'laziness.'

Often, we view laziness as the opposite of productivity, a trait to be frowned upon. However, what if I told you that within 'laziness' lies an untapped brilliance – a secret weapon for success and satisfaction? Welcome to the world of 'The Lazy Brilliance', a concept that turns traditional thinking on its head.

Let's start with a story that perfectly encapsulates this idea. There was a manager in a renowned company, known for his unconventional approach. While his peers clocked in extra hours, he seemed to work less, yet his team consistently outperformed others. His secret? He focused on 'smart work' rather than 'hard work'. He delegated effectively, prioritized tasks with precision, and encouraged regular breaks to rejuvenate his team's creativity. He was the embodiment of 'lazy brilliance' – achieving more by strategically doing less.

This story isn't unique. History is replete with examples of successful individuals who harnessed the power of 'lazy brilliance'. Take Albert Einstein, for instance. His daydreams and 'lazy hours' led to some of the most groundbreaking ideas in physics. His ability to embrace idleness allowed his mind the freedom to wander and explore the realms of imagination, leading to discoveries that changed our understanding of the universe.

So, what exactly is 'The Lazy Brilliance'? It's the art of maximizing efficiency by minimizing unnecessary effort. It's about finding the most effective, simplest route to achieve your goals. It's not about shunning work; it's about working smarter.

Research supports this approach. Studies have shown that overworking can lead to decreased productivity, impaired cognitive function, and a host of health issues. On the contrary, strategic breaks and a balanced work approach can boost creativity, improve problem-solving skills, and enhance overall productivity.

But how do you apply this in real life? It starts with redefining your approach to work and success. For instance, rather than measuring productivity by the number of hours worked, gauge it by the impact and quality of what you produce. Break down tasks into smaller, manageable parts and focus on one thing at a time. This method, often referred to as the 'Pomodoro Technique', involves working in short bursts followed by brief breaks. It's a practical application of 'lazy brilliance'.

Moreover, embrace the power of delegation. Many successful leaders, from business moguls to presidents, have mastered this art. They understand that you don't have to do everything yourself. By delegating tasks, you free up time to focus on what you do best, leading to better outcomes and a more balanced life.

In essence, 'The Lazy Brilliance' is about making your work life not just bearable, but enjoyable and effective. It's about finding the sweet spot where productivity and relaxation intersect. By embracing this philosophy, you'll not only achieve more but also find greater satisfaction in what you do.

As you continue reading, remember this: 'The Lazy Brilliance' isn't just a theory; it's a practical, life-changing approach that has been proven time and time again. It's your turn now to unlock this hidden potential and redefine what success means to you.

In the following chapters, we'll delve deeper into how you can apply 'The Lazy Brilliance' in various aspects of your life. From prioritizing tasks to mastering the art of 'strategic idleness', get ready to transform the way you work, think, and live. Welcome to a journey of discovering how doing less can mean achieving more.

Discover the hidden genius in laziness

The Misunderstood Virtue called laziness

Let's start by shattering a common myth: Laziness is not the enemy of success; misunderstood, it's often its secret ally. Think of some of the greatest minds – Albert Einstein, who famously said, "I am a lazy person," or Steve Jobs, known for his minimalist approach. Their laziness wasn't a lack of action; it was strategic, a choice to focus on what truly matters.

In our fast-paced world, being busy is often equated with being productive. But is it really? Countless people rush through tasks, filling every minute with activity, yet at day's end, they're left wondering, "What have I truly accomplished?"

The Power of Strategic Rest

Consider this: A study by the University of Illinois found that brief diversions from a task can dramatically improve one's ability to focus on that task for prolonged periods. In simple terms, strategic laziness – those moments of intentional inactivity – can recharge your brain, leading to more productive and creative work periods.

Real-Life Testimonials

Take Sarah, a software developer. Overwhelmed by her workload, she was constantly stressed, her productivity plummeting. Upon adopting the principles of 'productive laziness,' she began taking regular short breaks and focused only on the crucial aspects of her projects. The result? Higher quality work, completed faster, and a newfound sense of job satisfaction.

Or consider Mike, a school teacher, who always felt behind despite working late hours. He decided to implement 'laziness' into his schedule: more time for planning, less for unnecessary meetings, and regular pauses. His teaching became more impactful, and his students' performance improved.

The Art of Delegation and Automation

Delegation and automation are key components of finding genius in laziness. By intelligently outsourcing or automating menial tasks, you free up mental space for creativity and innovation. It's not about doing less work; it's about doing less unnecessary work.

The Link Between Laziness and Creativity

Some of the most creative ideas emerge in moments of idleness. When your mind is relaxed, it's free to wander, to explore, to connect disparate ideas – this is the bedrock of innovation. In fact, research suggests that daydreaming – an activity often associated with laziness – is an integral part of problem-solving and creative thinking.

Embracing Laziness as a Lifestyle

Adopting laziness as a lifestyle doesn't mean shirking responsibilities. It means redefining your approach to work and life. It's about finding balance, understanding your limits, and respecting your need for mental and physical rest.

In conclusion, the hidden genius in laziness is not a myth but a reality, backed by both anecdotal and scientific evidence. It's about working smarter, not harder. It's about understanding that sometimes, the best thing you can do for your productivity, creativity, and overall well-being is to simply... pause.

As you turn the page, remember: In the art of laziness lies the key to unlocking your fullest potential.

CHAPTER 2

Comfort Zone: Friend or Foe?

"A ship in harbor is safe, but that is not what ships are built for." – **John A. Shedd**

This familiar quote rings especially true when we consider the concept of the comfort zone in the context of "The Art of Laziness." At first glance, it might seem like the epitome of laziness is to remain in one's comfort zone – safe, unchallenged, and at ease. However, as we delve deeper, we discover that the true art of laziness isn't about staying static; it's about moving with purpose and ease.

The comfort zone is a tricky thing. It's like a cozy blanket on a cold morning – leaving it requires effort, but staying under it all day? That's not comfort; it's stagnation. The art of laziness doesn't advocate for a life spent in the shadows of the unchallenged and familiar. Instead, it encourages us to step out, but with an air of ease and confidence.

Think about some of the most successful people you know or have read about. Did they achieve their greatness by staying comfortable? In most cases, the answer is a resounding no. But here's where it gets interesting – their journey wasn't about pushing themselves relentlessly. It was about smart moves, about knowing when to step out of their comfort zone, and when to rest.

Take the example of a well-known entrepreneur who, instead of burning the midnight oil, chose to delegate tasks effectively. He stepped out of his comfort zone not by doing more, but by trusting others to help carry the load. This shift from a do-it-all mindset to a do-it-smart approach is at the heart of productive laziness.

Or consider the story of a writer who found her creative voice not by forcing herself to write more, but by giving herself the space to explore different genres. She stepped out of her comfort zone, not by writing more words, but by allowing herself to write different words.

In both cases, these individuals embraced the essence of productive laziness. They understood that their comfort zone, while safe, wasn't where growth happened. They also recognized that leaving it didn't mean a frantic dash into the unknown. It meant thoughtful, strategic steps towards growth, combined with the wisdom to know when rest was needed.

This section of the book is not about demonizing the comfort zone. It's about understanding its role. It's a starting point, a place of rest and rejuvenation. But it's not a place to set up permanent residence. The art of laziness is about finding a balance – knowing when to step out and take a risk, and when to step back and recharge.

As we explore this concept further, we'll delve into strategies for identifying when your comfort zone is serving you, and when it's holding you back. We'll discuss how to recognize the right moments to step out and how to do so in a way that aligns with the principles of productive laziness.

Remember, the goal is not constant motion, but purposeful action. It's about moving with intention, with an understanding that sometimes, the most productive thing you can do is to pause, reflect, and then proceed with clarity and confidence.

So, ask yourself: Is your comfort zone a friend that offers occasional shelter, or a foe that keeps you from exploring your true potential? The answer to this question is the first step in mastering the art of laziness

– the art of living a life that is as fulfilling as it is effortlessly efficient.

Rethinking where you're most at ease.

Rethinking your comfort zone means questioning the routines and patterns you've mistaken for the optimal way of living. It's about understanding that sometimes, the most comfortable choice isn't the one that involves the least effort, but the one that aligns with your natural rhythms and strengths.

Let's break it down:

1. **Identifying False Comfort**: Often, what we think is our comfort zone is actually a trap of our own making, one that limits our potential. It's about recognizing these traps - the overworking, the relentless pursuit of perfection, the fear of delegation - and understanding that they're not really comfortable, but restrictive.

2. **Embracing Strategic Discomfort**: It might sound counterintuitive, but occasionally stepping into discomfort can lead to greater ease in the long run. This could mean trying new approaches to work, allowing yourself to be 'imperfect', or even taking time off. It's in these

moments of discomfort that we often find new strengths and insights.

3. **The Real Comfort in Laziness**: The art of laziness isn't about idleness; it's about finding the most effective and least stressful way to achieve your goals. It's about aligning with your natural energy flows, understanding when to push and when to rest, and recognizing that sometimes, the best action is inaction.

4. **Practical Steps to Expand Your Comfort Zone**: Start small. Delegate a minor task, take a short break during your busiest time, or try a new method of problem-solving. Observe how these small changes impact your productivity and well-being.

In rethinking where you're most at ease, you'll find that the real comfort lies not in the familiar and the routine, but in the balanced, the strategic, and the peacefully productive. Welcome to a new understanding of comfort, where ease and achievement walk hand in hand. Welcome to the heart of "The Art of Laziness."

CHAPTER 3
Choosing What Matters
The art of prioritizing with ease

*"The key is not to prioritize what's on your schedule, but to schedule your priorities." - **Stephen Covey***

In a world full of endless tasks, distractions, and responsibilities, the ability to choose what truly matters can be your greatest superpower. This chapter isn't just about making lists or ticking off tasks; it's about rediscovering the art of prioritizing with an ease that may seem, at first glance, almost lazy. But as you'll soon realize, this 'laziness' is actually the wisest, most efficient strategy for a fulfilling life.

The Power of Selective Focus

Let's delve into the story of Emma, a successful entrepreneur who seemed to have it all – a thriving business, a loving family, and a buzzing social life. Yet, Emma felt overwhelmed and stretched thin. Her secret? She mastered the art of selective focus, a cornerstone of 'productive laziness'.

Emma's approach was simple: she spent her mornings identifying the one or two tasks that would make the most significant impact on her day. These weren't necessarily the most urgent tasks, but they were the ones that aligned most closely with her long-term goals and personal values. By focusing on these key tasks, Emma found that she could afford to be 'lazy' with less critical tasks, sometimes even neglecting them altogether. This selective focus wasn't a sign of irresponsibility; it was a strategic choice that led to greater productivity and personal satisfaction.

The Myth of Multi-Tasking

The myth of multitasking is a trap that many fall into. We live in a culture that celebrates the idea of doing multiple things at once. However, research shows that multitasking can reduce productivity by as much as 40%. It's not just about doing less; it's about doing what's important and doing it well.

Prioritizing with Ease: The 80/20 Rule

The 80/20 Rule, or Pareto Principle, is a powerful tool in the art of prioritizing. It suggests that 20% of your activities will account for 80% of your results. The trick lies in identifying that crucial 20%. It's about finding the tasks that yield the most significant results and giving them your undivided attention. This is where 'productive laziness' comes into play. It's about working smarter, not harder, and getting more done by focusing on less.

The Joy of Saying 'No'

One of the most liberating aspects of prioritizing is learning to say 'no'. It's about understanding that every time you say 'yes' to something, you're indirectly saying 'no' to something else – potentially something more important. Steve Jobs once said, "Focusing is about saying no." The art of laziness isn't about shirking responsibility; it's about being clear on what truly matters and having the courage to say no to the rest.

Practical Steps to Prioritize with Ease

1. **Identify Your High-Impact Tasks**: Each day, determine the one or two tasks that will make the most significant difference. Focus on these first.

2. **Apply the 80/20 Rule**: Regularly analyze your activities to identify the 20% that

contribute to 80% of your results. Focus your energy here.

3. **Embrace the Power of 'No'**: Be selective about the commitments you take on. If it doesn't align with your key priorities, be prepared to decline.

4. **Simplify Your To-Do List**: Instead of a long list of tasks, keep a concise list focused on impactful activities.

5. **Reflect and Adjust Regularly**: End each day with a reflection on what worked and what didn't. Adjust your approach accordingly.

By choosing what truly matters and permitting yourself to focus on these priorities, you'll find that 'being lazy' in this strategic way isn't just enjoyable – it's incredibly effective.

CHAPTER 4
Perfectly Imperfect
Why aiming for 'good enough' wins

"Perfection is the enemy of progress."

- *Winston Churchill*

In a world obsessed with perfection, where social media flaunts flawless lives and the media glorifies only the highest achievements, it's easy to fall into the trap of believing that anything less than perfect is not worth doing. We are conditioned to aim for the stars, to seek out the best in everything we do, and to criticize ourselves harshly for every small imperfection. But what if I told you that this relentless pursuit of perfection is not only futile but also detrimental to our happiness and success?

The Myth of Perfection

Let's start by debunking a common myth: perfection does not exist. Yes, you read that right. In every aspect of life, from art to science, from personal relationships to professional endeavors, there is no such thing as perfect. Even the most successful people have their flaws and shortcomings. The key difference is their acceptance of imperfection, not the absence of it.

Good Enough is Great

The concept of 'good enough' often gets a bad rap, dismissed as a form of laziness or lack of ambition. But let's redefine 'good enough' as a realistic, healthy standard that fosters progress and growth. 'Good enough' is not about mediocrity; it's about setting achievable goals, celebrating progress, and learning from failures.

The Paralysis of Perfectionism

Perfectionism can be paralyzing. The fear of not being perfect can stop us from starting a project, sharing our work, or trying something new. It creates a crippling fear of failure, where the only acceptable outcome is flawless success. This unrealistic expectation leads to procrastination, anxiety, and a host of other issues that hinder our ability to achieve and thrive.

Embracing the Flaws

There's beauty in imperfection. The Japanese art of Kintsugi, where broken pottery is repaired with gold, teaches us that there is elegance and history in the cracks and flaws. Similarly, embracing our imperfections in life and work can lead to a more authentic, fulfilling existence.

The Power of 'Good Enough'

Aiming for 'good enough' empowers us to take risks, try new things, and learn from our experiences. It encourages a growth mindset, where the focus is on the journey, not just the destination. It's about doing the best you can with what you have and then letting go.

The Liberation of Letting Go

Letting go of the need for perfection frees us from the shackles of unrealistic expectations. It allows us to be more creative, more adventurous, and more resilient. When we're not afraid to fail, we open ourselves up to a world of possibilities.

The Balance of 'Good Enough'

It's important to find the right balance. 'Good enough' doesn't mean giving up on improvement or settling for less. It means recognizing when the additional effort yields diminishing returns and focusing your energy where it counts most.

The Journey of Self-Acceptance

Embracing 'good enough' is also a journey of self-acceptance. It's understanding that you are a work in progress and that your worth is not defined by your achievements or lack thereof. It's about being kind to yourself and recognizing your efforts.

In the pursuit of happiness and success, let's shift our focus from the unattainable ideal of perfection to the achievable standard of 'good enough'. By doing so, we open the doors to a more balanced, joyful, and fulfilling life. Remember, in the art of living, as in the art of laziness, it is often the imperfect, the unfinished, and the good enough that bring the greatest joy and success.

As we conclude this chapter, let's reflect on the words of Leonard Cohen: *"There is a crack in everything. That's how the light gets in."* Embrace your imperfections, for they are not just cracks, but openings for growth, learning, and light.

CHAPTER 5
Simplicity in Action
Doing less but achieving more

"Simplicity is the ultimate sophistication."

– Leonardo da Vinci

What if I told you that the secret to greater achievement and to unlocking a more fulfilling life, lies in the art of doing less? Yes, that's right. Less, but with more intention, and more focus. This chapter is not just a set of instructions; it's a new lens through which to view your actions, your goals, and your life's trajectory.

The Irony of Effort

Imagine a river, flowing smoothly and unhindered towards the ocean. It does not strain, it does not rush, yet it reaches its destination with certainty. This is the essence of simplicity in action. The river, by doing less, achieves more. The paradox of effort is simple: the harder we try to force results, the more elusive they become.

Simplicity in Action: An Everyday Guide

1. **Identify the Essential**: Start by asking yourself, what is truly essential in your life? This

is not about material possessions alone but about activities, relationships, and goals. Strip away the unnecessary, and you'll find clarity and focus.

2. **Embrace the 'Less but Better' Philosophy**: Quality over quantity. It's about doing fewer things but doing them better. This approach leads to higher productivity, more satisfaction, and a deeper sense of accomplishment.

3. **Automate and Delegate**: In today's world, technology and collaboration are your allies. Automate the mundane, delegate the non-essential, and free up your time for what truly matters.

4. **Practice Mindfulness**: Be present in everything you do. Mindfulness leads to better decisions, higher efficiency, and a deeper connection with your work and those around you.

5. **Set Limits**: Constraints breed creativity. Set time limits for tasks, limit the number of

projects you undertake, and watch as your efficiency soars.

6. **Rest is a Weapon**: Never underestimate the power of rest. A well-rested mind is more creative, more analytical, and more efficient.

The Art of Achieving More by Doing Less

Here we delve deeper into the philosophy of achieving more by doing less. It's about leveraging the power of focused effort, strategic inaction, and the wisdom of knowing when to step back.

The case study of a Farmer and his Field

There was once a farmer who believed in working his field from dawn till dusk. Despite his hard work, his yield was mediocre. His neighbor, who worked less but with strategic planning, always had a bountiful harvest. The secret? Understanding the rhythm of the seasons, the field's need for rest, and the right time for action.

Mastering Strategic Inactivity

1. **Prioritize Your Tasks**: Understand the difference between urgent and important. Focus on what brings the greatest reward for the least effort.

2. **The Power of 'No'**: Saying no is an art. It's about protecting your time, energy, and focus for what truly matters.

3. **Leverage the Compound Effect**: Small, consistent actions over time yield massive results. It's not about big leaps but about incremental, sustained efforts.

4. **Embrace Rest and Reflection**: Often, stepping back gives you a clearer view. Rest and reflection are not just about recovery; they are tools for strategic planning and creative thinking.

5. **Learn from Nature**: Nature does not hurry, yet everything is accomplished. Observe the rhythm of nature and apply it to your work and life.

6. **Quality Over Speed**: In our rush to get things done, we often sacrifice quality. Slow down. Excellence lies in attention to detail.

By adopting the principles of simplicity in action and doing less to achieve more, you open doors to a more productive, fulfilling, and enlightened way of life.

CHAPTER 6
Routine Reimagined
Crafting a day for the effortlessly efficient

"Routine reimagined is not about stringent schedules, but about crafting a day for the effortlessly efficient, where every moment is a step towards a more fulfilling life."

- *Jordan Peterson*

This chapter isn't just about setting alarms or brewing the perfect cup of coffee; it's about understanding the hidden rhythm of your day and aligning it with your deepest aspirations.

As the first light of daybreak pierces the horizon, there's an unsung symphony that plays, a melody of potential and promise. The morning, often rushed through or slept past, holds within it an unspoken power. The key lies not in overloading these precious hours with tasks but in crafting them with an intention that sets the tone for the day.

Think about it. How often have we been told that the early bird catches the worm? Yet, this isn't about being early; it's about being intentional. What if, instead of chasing the worm, we focus on understanding the field, the environment where the worm thrives? It's about knowing your field – your life, your aspirations, your strengths – and aligning your morning with this knowledge.

The Myth of the Perfect Routine (tailored to your specification)

Let's debunk a myth here: There is no one-size-fits-all morning routine. The glorified routines of CEOs and celebrities splashed across magazine pages are not the secret elixir to your efficiency. Your routine should be as unique as your fingerprint. It's about understanding your rhythms, your energy ebb and flow, and crafting a routine that respects and harnesses these natural patterns.

What does that look like? It could be starting your day with a ten-minute meditation, a brisk walk, or simply sitting in silence with your thoughts. The activity itself is secondary; the primary focus is on creating a space where you align your thoughts with your actions for the day.

The Beauty in Minimalism

Minimalism in your morning routine isn't about depriving yourself; it's about enriching your focus. Choose one or two key activities that ground you, activities that give you clarity and calm. It could be as simple as making your bed, a small act that sets the tone for a day of completed tasks, or a few moments of gratitude, acknowledging the good that already exists in your life.

Remember, the goal of your morning isn't to conquer the world; it's to set the stage for a day where you are at your best, a day where you navigate through tasks with ease and grace.

The Ritual of Reflection

One of the most powerful tools in your morning arsenal is reflection. Take a few moments each morning to reflect on the day ahead. What are the key tasks? What challenges might arise? How do you want to feel at the end of the day? This isn't about detailed planning; it's about setting your internal compass in the right direction.

As you pour your morning beverage, let that act serve as a reminder to pour into yourself too, to fill your own cup with intention and awareness. As you sip, ponder on the day ahead, and visualize yourself moving through it with ease and efficiency.

The art of laziness, contrary to its name, isn't about doing nothing. It's about doing what matters, in the most efficient way possible. It's about understanding that sometimes, the best action is inaction. By crafting a morning routine that aligns with your natural rhythms, you are setting yourself up for a day of effortless efficiency.

As you step into the rest of your day, carry with you the calm and focus of your morning. Let it be a reminder that in the quiet, in the simplicity of your routine, lies your power. Your morning isn't just the start of your day; it's the foundation of a life lived with intention, ease, and efficiency.

Understanding the Rhythm of Your Day

Every day has its own rhythm, a unique pulse that, if listened to, can guide you to your most productive and fulfilling moments. It's essential to recognize these rhythms and align your activities accordingly. Some of us are at our peak in the morning, others in the afternoon, and some in the quiet of the night. The key is not to fight these natural inclinations but to embrace and work with them.

Take a moment to reflect: When do you feel most energetic? When do you feel most creative? Schedule your most demanding tasks during these peaks. Place less demanding, more routine tasks in your less energetic periods. This alignment creates a flow that feels natural and effortless.

The Art of Prioritization

The cornerstone of an efficiently crafted day lies in prioritization. It's not about doing more; it's about doing what matters. Ask yourself, "What are the three most important tasks today?" Focus on these. Completing these key tasks will give you a sense of accomplishment and reduce the stress of an overwhelming to-do list.

Remember, it's okay to say no. Part of crafting an efficiently lazy day is understanding that you can't do everything, and more importantly, you shouldn't. Focus on what aligns with your goals and values, and let go of the rest.

Strategic Laziness

Strategic laziness is an art form. It's about finding smarter ways to do tasks, ways that require less effort but yield high results. Automate where you can. Delegate tasks that don't require your unique skill set. Use technology to your advantage. The goal is to reduce unnecessary effort so that you can focus on what truly matters.

The Power of Breaks

Never underestimate the power of a well-timed break. The human mind wasn't designed to focus for long stretches without rest. Incorporate short, regular breaks throughout your day. A five-minute walk, a moment of stretching, or simply stepping away from your workspace can rejuvenate your mind and increase your productivity.

Ending Your Day with Intention

As your day winds down, it's important to have a closing ritual, a way to signal to your brain that the workday is over. It could be a simple act like shutting down your computer or a moment of reflection on the day's achievements. This helps create a clear boundary between work and rest, allowing you to fully disengage and recharge for the next day.

As we conclude this chapter, remember that crafting a day for the effortlessly efficient isn't about rigid structures or packed schedules. It's about understanding your rhythms, prioritizing what matters, and moving through your day with a sense of ease and intention. In the next chapter, we'll explore how to carry this philosophy into your personal life, creating a balance that allows you to thrive both professionally and personally.

Stay tuned for a journey into harmonizing work and life, where the art of laziness becomes not just a practice but a way of being.

CHAPTER 7
The Power of 'No'
A simple word for a simpler life

"The difference between successful people and really successful people is that really successful people say no to almost everything." - **Warren Buffett**

No is the gatekeeper to a life less cluttered, a mindless burdened, and a schedule less overwhelming. Yet, many of us struggle to utter it. We fear missing out, disappointing others, or appearing selfish. But herein lies the paradox: saying 'No' is not about closing doors; it's about opening the right ones.

The Cult of Busyness

We live in a society that glorifies busyness. Being busy is often equated with being important, productive, and successful. But is it, really? How many of our 'yeses' lead to meaningful achievements, and how many simply add to the noise, the stress, and the endless to-do lists that dominate our lives?

The Power of 'No'

Saying 'No' is an act of self-preservation. It's about recognizing and honoring our limits. Every time we say 'No' to something that doesn't align with our priorities or values, we say 'Yes' to something that does. It's a conscious choice to focus on what truly matters.

The Art of Declining

The art of saying 'No' isn't about being rude or dismissive. It's about being honest and respectful - to ourselves and others. It's about understanding that our time and energy are finite resources and that we have the right to allocate them as we see fit.

The Ripple Effect of 'No'

When we start saying 'No', something remarkable happens. We find more time for our passions, our loved ones, and ourselves. We become more present, less stressed, and ironically, more productive in the things that matter most. Our 'No' can inspire others to reassess their own choices, creating a ripple effect of positive change.

Saying 'No' is a critical tool in this approach. It's about consciously choosing a path of less resistance and greater joy.

Below is the power behind 'No' towards a life of liberating laziness.

1. Reclaiming Your Time

Every 'No' is a step towards reclaiming your time. Time is the one resource we cannot replenish. By saying 'No' to things that don't serve your purpose or bring you joy, you are effectively prioritizing your time for what truly matters. This is not laziness; it's smart allocation of your most precious resource.

2. Reducing Stress and Overwhelm

The inability to say 'No' is a direct route to stress and overwhelm. When we overcommit, we spread ourselves thin, and our quality of life deteriorates. Embracing 'No' allows us to set healthy boundaries. This boundary-setting is an act of self-care, ensuring we don't burn out in our attempt to meet external expectations.

3. Enhancing Focus and Productivity

Paradoxically, the art of saying 'No' can lead to enhanced productivity. By declining commitments that aren't aligned with our goals, we free up mental space and energy. This newfound focus allows us to excel in the activities we do choose to pursue. It's about doing less but achieving more.

4. Cultivating Authentic Relationships

Saying 'No' also fosters authenticity in relationships. When we stop saying 'Yes' to please others and start being true to our own needs and desires, our relationships become more genuine. We connect with people on a deeper level, based on mutual respect and understanding of boundaries.

5. Encouraging Self-Discovery

Every time you say 'No' to something that doesn't align with your values, you learn more about what does. This process of elimination is a journey of self-discovery. You get to understand what truly motivates you, what your passions are, and what kind of life you genuinely want to lead.

As you navigate through "The Art of Laziness," remember that saying 'No' is not a sign of weakness or selfishness. It's a powerful statement of self-awareness and self-respect. It's about making choices that align with your true self, leading to a simpler, more intentional, and ultimately more satisfying life. Let the power of 'No' be your guide in this journey towards a life of liberating laziness.

CHAPTER 8
Rest to Progress
Why non-stop working doesn't work

*"Rest is not idleness, and to lie sometimes on the grass under trees on a summer's day, listening to the murmur of the water, or watching the clouds float across the sky, is by no means a waste of time." - **John Lubbock***

Have you ever felt the world spinning relentlessly as you stand still? That gnawing guilt of taking a break while others seemingly march tirelessly forward? This chapter invites you on a journey to explore an often-misunderstood ally in our quest for success: Rest.

Imagine a world where the measure of success isn't the hours, we grind but the quality of what we produce. It sounds revolutionary, almost rebellious, in a society that glorifies the 'hustle culture'. But let's delve deeper, beyond the superficial glorification of non-stop work, and uncover why rest is not just a luxury but a necessity for progress.

Rest is often painted as the antithesis of productivity, a siren luring us away from our goals. However, the reality is startlingly different. Rest is the secret ingredient in the recipe for sustainable success.

Consider the analogy of an archer. To shoot an arrow, the archer must pull back the string with just the right amount of tension. Too little, and the arrow falls short; too much, and the string might snap. The art of resting is akin to finding that perfect tension. It's about pulling back just enough to catapult ourselves forward with greater force and accuracy.

In our relentless pursuit of productivity, we've fallen into the trap of believing that more hours equate to more output. But, research begs to differ. Studies show that excessive work leads to burnout, reduced quality of output, and even health issues. It's a diminishing return on investment.

Rest isn't about lounging on a couch aimlessly. It's an active state where you allow your mind and body to rejuvenate. It's giving yourself permission to step back, so when you return to your work, you're sharper, more creative, and more efficient.

The art of laziness, as paradoxical as it may sound, is about mastering the art of rest. It's about understanding that to move forward, sometimes you need to stand still. It's recognizing that the greatest ideas often come not in the whirlwind of activity but in the quiet moments of relaxation.

Let's debunk the myth that non-stop working equates to success. History is replete with examples of great minds who valued rest. Thomas Edison, known for his tireless work ethic, was also a proponent of short naps to recharge his mind. Winston Churchill, while leading a country through war, insisted on his afternoon siesta.

In this chapter, we'll explore how rest plays a crucial role in enhancing creativity, problem-solving abilities, and overall well-being. We'll discover strategies to integrate effective rest into our daily lives and understand why taking a break isn't just a pause in our journey to success but a vital part of it.

As you turn these pages, remember that every word here is an invitation to rethink, reset, and embrace the art of laziness as a tool for progress. The guilt of resting is a societal construct, a chain that binds our true potential. Breaking free from this mindset isn't just liberating; it's essential.

The journey ahead is not just about learning to rest but about redefining our relationship with work and success. It's about realizing that in the symphony of life, the pauses are as important as the notes.

So, as we dive into the depths of 'Rest to Progress', let's keep an open mind. Let's challenge the status quo and rediscover the power of slowing down. For in the art of laziness lies the secret to our greatest achievements.

Practical ways rest improves creativity, problem-solving skills, and general well-being let's delve into practical ways in which rest enhances creativity, problem-solving abilities, and overall well-being. This journey is not just about understanding the theory but also about applying it to our daily lives.

Creativity Unleashed

Creativity thrives in a relaxed state of mind. It's like a shy deer that appears only when the forest is quiet. The constant grind of work can be the noise that scares it away. But how do we create this quiet forest in our busy lives?

1. **Structured Daydreaming**: Allocate time for structured daydreaming. This isn't aimless wandering of thoughts but a conscious decision to let your mind roam freely around a specific

problem or idea. Albert Einstein famously used daydreaming to develop his theory of relativity.

2. **Nature Therapy**: Spend time in nature. Nature has a calming effect on the mind, which can lead to a surge in creativity. A simple walk in the park, listening to the birds, and feeling the breeze, can open up a wellspring of ideas.

3. **Diverse Hobbies**: Engage in hobbies unrelated to your work. Hobbies can stimulate different parts of your brain, leading to a cross-pollination of ideas. The famous inventor Alexander Graham Bell was also an avid kite-maker, which influenced his scientific work.

Enhancing Problem-Solving Abilities

Problem-solving is not just about working hard on a problem but also about working smart. And sometimes, working smart means taking a step back.

1. **Sleep on It**: Never underestimate the power of a good night's sleep. Sleep is a powerful tool for cognitive processing. It's during sleep that our brain sorts, processes, and connects information, leading to 'eureka' moments upon waking.

2. **Meditation and Mindfulness**: Practice meditation and mindfulness. These practices clear the mental clutter, allowing us to approach problems with a fresh perspective. Even a few minutes a day can significantly improve our problem-solving capabilities.

3. **Switch Tasks**: If you're stuck on a problem, switch tasks. Engaging in a different activity can give your subconscious mind time to work on the problem in the background, often leading to unexpected solutions.

Boosting Overall Well-Being

Lastly, let's not forget the overarching umbrella of well-being. A well-rested individual is more likely to be a happy, healthy, and productive individual.

1. **Regular Breaks**: Incorporate regular breaks into your daily routine. Use techniques like the Pomodoro Technique, where you work for 25 minutes and then take a 5-minute break.

2. **Social Connections**: Spend quality time with friends and family. Social connections can provide emotional rest, which is just as important as physical rest.

3. **Mindful Eating and Exercise**: Pay attention to your diet and exercise. A healthy body supports a healthy mind. Even light exercise like stretching or yoga can be incredibly restorative.

By integrating these practices into our lives, we begin to experience the transformative power of rest. It's not about being lazy in the traditional sense but about being strategically lazy. It's about understanding that the best way to move forward sometimes is to step back.

As you implement these strategies, observe the changes in your creativity, problem-solving abilities, and overall well-being. The journey of embracing the art of laziness is unique for each individual, but the destination is invariably a more fulfilled, productive, and creative life.

CHAPTER 9
Delaying the Inevitable?
Tackling procrastination head-on.

"Procrastination is the thief of time, collar him." –
Charles Dickens

In the web of our daily lives, where tasks loom like minotaurs, we often find ourselves at a crossroads. Here, we face a choice: to tackle the beast head-on or to retreat into the comforting shadows of delay. This chapter delves into the art of delaying the inevitable, a practice as common as it is misunderstood.

The Trap of Tomorrow

Why do we procrastinate? The answer lies not in laziness, as commonly misconceived, but in the intricate workings of the human psyche. Our brains are wired to prioritize immediate comfort over long-term benefits, a trait inherited from our ancestors who lived in a world where immediate action often meant survival. In the modern era, this translates into putting off tasks that seem daunting, uncomfortable, or simply tedious.

The Cost of Waiting

Delay comes at a price. The stress of unfinished tasks accumulates like interest on an unpaid debt, weighing down on our mental well-being. This perpetual state of 'planning to do' creates a cycle of anxiety and avoidance. We become trapped in a paradox: seeking comfort in delay, yet finding none as the shadow of the unaccomplished grows longer.

Tackling Procrastination Head-On

Confronting procrastination is akin to facing our own Goliath. It requires a blend of self-awareness, strategy, and a sprinkle of audacity. The first step is recognition - acknowledging that procrastination is not a character flaw, but a common human behavior that can be managed.

Strategies to Overcome Procrastination

1. **Start Small:** Break your task into smaller, manageable parts. The first step doesn't have to be grand; it just needs to be.

2. **Set Clear Deadlines:** Ambiguity is the ally of delay. Clear, tangible deadlines create a sense of urgency and accountability.

3. **Understand Your Why:** Connect with the purpose behind the task. Why is it important? How does it align with your values and goals?

4. **Create a Productive Environment:** Your surroundings should encourage work, not hinder it. Eliminate distractions that tempt you into procrastinating.

5. **Reward Progress:** Reinforce positive behavior by rewarding yourself for meeting small milestones.

6. **Forgive Yourself:** Procrastination is a common human behavior. Beating yourself up only leads to more avoidance. Practice self-compassion and understand that it's okay to stumble.

7. **Seek Accountability:** Share your goals with someone who can hold you accountable. Sometimes, knowing that someone else is watching can be a powerful motivator.

The Power of Now

Embracing the present moment is a potent antidote to procrastination. Often, the hardest part is not the task itself, but starting it. Committing to just five minutes of work can break the inertia, turning dread into momentum. This technique, surprisingly simple yet effective, is known as the 'Five Minute Miracle.'

Rewiring for Reward

Human behavior is largely driven by the pursuit of reward. By redefining the rewards of task completion – be it the satisfaction of crossing it off a list, the joy of accomplishment, or the relief of avoiding last-minute panic – we can shift our perspective from avoidance to anticipation.

Delaying the inevitable is a dance with time – one that can be graceful when done with awareness and strategy. As we navigate the waters of procrastination, let us remember that the art of doing lies not in perfection, but in progress. In the words of Karen Lamb, "A year from now you may wish you had started today."

CHAPTER 10
Your Circle of Calm

*"In the midst of movement and chaos, keep stillness inside of you." - **Deepak Chopra***

In our relentless pursuit of productivity, we've forgotten the art of stillness, the luxury of doing nothing. Welcome to "Your Circle of Calm," where we rediscover tranquility amidst our chaotic lives. This isn't about encouraging idleness; it's about embracing a different kind of activity - the activity of calm.

Imagine a world where stillness is your superpower. It's not the lack of action; it's a deliberate pause, a chosen silence that recharges your mind and soul. This chapter isn't just a series of words; it's a journey into the heart of tranquility, a guide to creating your personal oasis of peace.

Understanding Your Circle

Your Circle of Calm is not a physical space; it's a mental sanctuary that you carry within yourself. It's where you retreat to find clarity and peace, away from the noise and haste of everyday life. But how do you find this circle? It begins with understanding the essence of calm. It's more than just relaxation; it's a state of being present, aware, and untroubled by the chaos that surrounds you.

Creating Your Circle

1. **Embrace Minimalism**: Start by decluttering your physical and mental space. A cluttered environment often leads to a cluttered mind. Embrace the principle of less is more.

2. **Practice Mindfulness**: Engage in activities that foster mindfulness, such as meditation, yoga, or simply taking a peaceful walk. The key is to be fully present in the moment.

3. **Set Boundaries**: Learn to say no. Your time and energy are precious. Guard them by setting healthy boundaries with work, technology, and even social obligations.

4. **Cultivate Quiet Times**: Dedicate a few minutes each day to sit in silence. It could be early in the morning or late at night. Use this time to reflect, meditate, or just breathe.

Living Within Your Circle

Now that you've created your circle, how do you live within it? It's about making conscious choices every day.

- **Start Your Day Calmly**: Avoid rushing into your day. Begin with a calm ritual, whether it's a cup of tea, a few minutes of stretching, or writing in a journal.

- **Mindful Interactions**: Engage with others mindfully. Listen more, speak less, and be fully present in your interactions.

- **Unplug Regularly**: Take breaks from digital devices. Digital detoxes, even short ones, can significantly reduce stress.

- **Embrace Nature**: Spend time in nature. The natural world has a calming effect on the mind and soul.

Surrounding yourself with ease and inspiration is about creating an environment that nurtures your spirit and encourages your growth. This chapter delves into how the company you keep and the environment you cultivate can impact your journey toward tranquility and inspiration.

The Environment You Create Is the Life You Live

The spaces we inhabit and the people we surround ourselves with have a profound impact on our mental and emotional well-being. This chapter is a guide to creating an environment that not only brings ease but also inspires you to be your best self.

Cultivating an Inspiring Environment

1. **Choose Your Company Wisely**: Surround yourself with positive, supportive people. Seek out those who inspire you, challenge you, and make you feel valued.

2. **Create a Personal Sanctuary**: Your home should be a refuge that reflects your personal

taste and promotes peace. Use colors, textures, and objects that bring you joy.

3. **Incorporate Elements of Nature**: Plants, natural light, and elements of water can create a soothing atmosphere. They also have health benefits, like purifying the air and reducing stress.

4. **Designate a Creative Space**: Have a space dedicated to creativity, whether it's for writing, painting, crafting, or just daydreaming.

Living in an Environment of Ease and Inspiration

- **Routine Rejuvenation**: Establish routines that rejuvenate you. This could be a weekly hobby, a reading hour, or a regular meetup with friends.

- **Constant Learning**: Keep your mind active and inspired by learning new things. Attend workshops, read books, or explore new hobbies.

- **Gratitude Practice**: Cultivate a habit of gratitude. Acknowledge and appreciate the good in your life, however small.

- **Balanced Lifestyle**: Strive for balance in your work, leisure, and relationships. Avoid extremes and find a harmonious rhythm in your daily life.

Remember, creating Your Circle of Calm and surrounding yourself with ease and inspiration is a personal journey. It's about finding what resonates with you, what brings you peace, and what inspires your soul.

CHAPTER 11
First Challenges, Then Ease
Starting with the hard-to-make-life-easy

*"Great works are performed not by strength but by perseverance." – **Samuel Johnson***

Have you ever wondered how the laziest people often seem to have the easiest lives? Counterintuitive, isn't it? But there's a secret to their ease, a method to their madness that's rarely understood but often desired. This chapter delves into that paradox – how facing challenges head-on can pave the way for a life of ease.

The Irony of Effort and Ease

In a world that glorifies the hustle, it's easy to overlook the power of strategic laziness. The art of laziness isn't about shirking responsibilities; it's about embracing challenges upfront to unlock a simpler, more efficient way of living.

Think of it as a computer algorithm. The most effective algorithms are those that tackle complex calculations early on, simplifying the rest of the process. Our lives are not much different. By addressing the hardest tasks at the outset, we set a foundation for a smoother, more streamlined existence.

The Illusion of the Easy Path

Many of us are tempted to choose the path of least resistance. It's human nature to avoid discomfort. However, this approach often leads to a life filled with unaddressed challenges, half-completed tasks, and a constant sense of playing catch-up.

Conversely, embracing the difficult tasks first can seem daunting. But this approach holds a secret: it builds resilience and efficiency. When you tackle the toughest challenges first, everything else seems easier in comparison. This strategy breeds a sense of accomplishment and momentum, making the subsequent tasks feel less burdensome.

Real-Life Examples of Strategic Laziness

Consider the story of Thomas, a software engineer. He chose to automate the most tedious parts of his job early in his career. This upfront effort seemed overwhelming at first, but it eventually freed up countless hours, allowing him to focus on more creative and rewarding aspects of his work.

Similarly, Maria, a school teacher, decided to invest her initial efforts in creating a comprehensive lesson plan and classroom management system. This upfront investment paid dividends throughout the school year, reducing her daily preparation time and increasing her effectiveness in teaching.

The Psychological Benefits

Engaging with challenges first not only streamlines your life but also enhances your mental wellbeing. It cultivates a growth mindset, where obstacles are viewed as opportunities for development rather than insurmountable barriers.

This proactive approach also reduces anxiety. Knowing that the most challenging part of your day is behind you brings a sense of relief and accomplishment, making the rest of your day more enjoyable and relaxed.

Practical Steps to Embrace Challenges

1. **Prioritize Your Tasks:** Start your day by identifying the most challenging task and tackle it first. This sets the tone for a productive day.

2. **Break It Down:** Large tasks can be overwhelming. Break them into smaller, manageable parts to avoid feeling daunted.

3. **Celebrate Small Victories:** Acknowledge and celebrate your progress. This builds momentum and encourages you to keep going.

4. **Reflect on the Benefits:** Regularly remind yourself of the long-term benefits of facing challenges upfront. This helps maintain motivation.

CHAPTER 12
Delegate to Elevate
Sharing tasks for shared success

*"The best way to find yourself is to lose yourself in the service of others." – **Mahatma Gandhi***

In the heart of every thriving organization, community, or family, lies a hidden, often underappreciated art - the art of delegation. This chapter, "Delegate to Elevate - Sharing Tasks for Shared Success," is not just a mere collection of words; it's a journey into the profound depths of leadership and personal growth. Here, we unravel how delegation is not a sign of weakness, but a symbol of strength and intelligence.

The Irony of Laziness

Imagine a world where 'laziness' is not a derogatory term, but a strategic approach to achieving more by doing less. Yes, you read that right - doing less. But how? The answer lies in the power of delegation. The true essence of 'laziness' in leadership is the artful and intelligent delegation of tasks. It's about recognizing that you don't have to be the one juggling all the balls. Instead, you can be the conductor of an orchestra, where each musician plays their part to create a harmonious symphony.

Why Delegate?

Delegation goes beyond simply offloading tasks; it's about empowerment. It's about entrusting your team with responsibilities and allowing them to grow, learn, and contribute meaningfully. When you delegate, you create a culture of trust and collaboration, where every member feels valued and integral to the team's success.

However, delegation is not without its challenges. The fear of losing control, worry about the quality of work, and the hesitation to rely on others can be daunting. However, these fears often stem from a lack of understanding of the delegation process and its benefits.

The Art of Delegating Effectively

To delegate effectively, start by identifying the right tasks to delegate. These are typically tasks that others can do or tasks that provide growth opportunities for your team. Then, choose the right people for these tasks. Look for individuals whose skills and interests align with the task at hand.

Once you've assigned the task, provide clear instructions and the necessary resources. Set expectations, but also give your team the freedom to approach the task in their own way. This autonomy is crucial for fostering innovation and ownership.

Most importantly, be available for guidance and support, but resist the urge to micromanage. Trust your team and their capabilities. Remember, delegation is a skill, and like all skills, it requires practice and patience to master.

Shared Success: The Ultimate Reward

When delegation is done right, it leads to shared success. Your team's achievements become your achievements. Their growth contributes to the growth of the entire organization. This shared success fosters a positive and productive work environment, where everyone feels a sense of purpose and belonging.

The Transformative Power of Delegation

Delegation is more than a management tactic; it's a transformative tool for personal and professional development. It frees up your time to focus on higher-level tasks, like strategy and vision. It also helps you develop your leadership skills, as you learn to guide, mentor, and inspire your team.

"Delegate to Elevate - Sharing Tasks for Shared Success" is not just a principle for effective leadership; it's a mantra for a fulfilling life. By mastering the art of delegation, you elevate not just yourself but those around you. You create a legacy of empowerment, collaboration, and success.

So, as you turn the pages of this chapter, reflect on how you can apply the art of delegation in your life. Embrace the 'laziness' that leads to greatness. Remember, the journey to the top is not a solo climb; it's a group hike, where every member plays a pivotal role. Delegate, elevate, and watch as you and your team soar to new heights. Let me end with this African proverb; *"If you want to go fast, go alone. If you want to go far, go together."*

CHAPTER 13
Learn Like a Pro

*"Learning like a pro isn't just about diligence; it's about smart strategies. Quick and easy learning techniques, such as active recall and spaced repetition, transform the complexity of knowledge into manageable, digestible pieces, enabling a seamless integration of new information." - **Barbara Oakley**

The term 'laziness' often carries a negative connotation, conjuring images of idleness and procrastination. However, when approached with mindfulness and strategy, what many deem laziness can actually be a powerful tool in learning. The essence of this approach lies in working smarter, not harder. By optimizing our learning methods, we can achieve more with less effort - a concept that appeals to the inherent desire for efficiency in all of us.

The Science Behind Efficient Learning

Recent advancements in cognitive science and psychology provide valuable insights into how we learn best. Studies show that our brains are not designed for long hours of monotonous study. Instead, they thrive on variety, short bursts of focused effort, and ample rest. Techniques such as spaced repetition, the

Pomodoro Technique, and interleaved learning capitalize on these principles, making learning more effective and less time-consuming.

Spaced Repetition: A Game Changer

Spaced repetition is a learning technique where information is reviewed at increasing intervals. This method leverages the psychological spacing effect, ensuring long-term retention with minimal effort. Tools like Anki and Quizlet make it easier to implement this strategy in daily study routines.

The Pomodoro Technique: Short Bursts of Focus

Developed by Francesco Cirillo, the Pomodoro Technique involves breaking work into short, timed intervals (traditionally 25 minutes in length) followed by short breaks. This keeps the brain fresh and maintains high levels of focus throughout a study session.

Interwoven Learning: Mixing It Up

Interleaving involves studying a mix of different subjects or topics in one session. This technique contrasts with block learning, where one topic is studied exhaustively in a single session. Interleaving strengthens cognitive abilities by teaching the brain to differentiate and adapt to various concepts simultaneously.

Practical Tips for Lazy Learning

1. **Use Technology Wisely**: Embrace apps and tools that facilitate efficient learning. From flashcard apps to online courses that use adaptive learning algorithms, technology can be a lazy learner's best friend.

2. **Focus on the Big Picture**: Prioritize learning concepts over memorizing facts. Understanding underlying principles makes it easier to apply knowledge in different contexts.

3. **Rest is Productive**: Never underestimate the power of a good night's sleep and regular breaks. Rest is crucial for memory consolidation and mental performance.

4. **Active Learning Over Passive Reading**: Engage with the material. Instead of just reading, try teaching the concept to someone else, or apply it in a practical project.

5. **Set Realistic Goals**: Break down your learning objectives into manageable chunks. Smaller goals are less daunting and easier to achieve.

Quick and Easy Learning Techniques
The Rapid Learning Mindset

Quick and easy learning is not just about the methods you use; it's also about the mindset. Adopting a growth mindset, where challenges are seen as opportunities to improve, is fundamental. This mindset, coupled with effective techniques, can significantly enhance learning efficiency.

The Feynman Technique: Simplify and Understand

Named after the Nobel Prize-winning physicist Richard Feynman, this technique involves explaining a concept in simple terms. If you can't explain it simply, you don't understand it well enough. This method forces you to break down complex ideas into their basic components, ensuring deep understanding and easier recall.

Focus on What Matters

Also known as the Pareto Principle, this rule suggests that roughly 80% of outcomes come from 20% of efforts. Identify the key 20% of your study material that will contribute the most to your understanding or performance in a subject, and focus your efforts there.

Mind Mapping: Visualize to Memorize

Mind mapping is a technique that involves creating a visual diagram of information. It helps in organizing and connecting ideas, making it easier to recall and understand complex subjects.

Speed Reading: Cover More in Less Time

While speed reading techniques vary, the core idea remains the same: increase the amount of text you can process at a time. Techniques like minimizing subvocalization and using a pointer to guide your eyes can significantly increase your reading speed.

Integrating Techniques into Daily Learning

1. **Create a Routine**: Establish a dedicated study routine that incorporates these techniques. Consistency is key.

2. **Customize Your Learning**: Adapt these techniques to fit your personal learning style and the subject matter.

3. **Practice Regularly**: Techniques like speed reading and mind mapping require practice to be effective.

4. **Stay Curious and Flexible**: Always be open to new methods and ideas that can enhance your learning experience.

5. **Measure Your Progress**: Regularly assess your understanding and skill development to ensure that these techniques are working for you.

In embracing the 'art of laziness', we discover that efficiency and relaxation are not mutually exclusive. By learning like a pro and adopting quick and easy learning techniques, we can achieve our educational goals with less stress and more enjoyment. This journey is not just about acquiring knowledge faster; it's about redefining our relationship with learning and embracing a more balanced and fulfilling approach to personal and professional development.

PART 2

LAZY YET EFFECTIVE TECHNIQUES

CHAPTER 14
20 Life-Changing Lazy Habits

"Small steps can lead to major impacts. It's about changing one lazy habit at a time, to transform your life."

- James Clear

Adopting lazy habits might seem counterintuitive when it comes to improving one's life. However, certain 'lazy' habits can actually lead to more significant accomplishments and a better quality of life. This chapter explores 20 lazy habits that can have a profound impact on your daily routine and overall well-being.

1. **Simplify Your Decisions**: Reduce the number of decisions you make daily. This can mean planning your meals for the week in advance or adopting a more uniform style of dressing. Decision fatigue is real, and simplifying choices can preserve mental energy for more critical tasks.

2. **Batch Processing Tasks**: Group similar tasks and do them in a single batch. This approach reduces the time spent switching between tasks and increases efficiency.

3. **Set Realistic Goals**: Setting achievable, realistic goals ensures that you don't get overwhelmed. It's better to succeed at smaller tasks than to fail at grandiose plans.

4. **Limit Time on Tasks**: By setting a time limit on tasks, you force yourself to focus and be more efficient. This is known as the Pomodoro Technique, where work is broken into intervals, traditionally 25 minutes in length, separated by short breaks.

5. **Practice Saying No**: Learn to decline requests that do not align with your priorities. It's a powerful way to conserve your time and energy for what truly matters.

6. **Take Regular Breaks**: Regular breaks enhance overall productivity and creativity. A short walk, a nap, or just stepping away from your workspace can rejuvenate your mind.

7. **Listen to Your Body**: If you're feeling tired or uninspired, listen to your body. Sometimes the best way to be productive is to take a rest or get more sleep.

8. **Leverage Tools and Resources**: Always be on the lookout for tools and resources that can make your tasks easier. This could mean using a new software tool, hiring a virtual assistant, or utilizing online services.

9. **Embrace Minimalism**: Reducing clutter and excess in your life can lead to a more focused and less stressful existence. This applies to physical items, digital clutter, and even social commitments.

10. **Prioritize Quality Over Quantity**: Focus on doing fewer things but with greater quality. This can apply to work, relationships, hobbies, and personal development.

11. **Develop Routines**: Establish routines for your most common tasks. Routines reduce the need for decision-making and can make tasks more automatic and less draining.

12. **Use Deadlines Effectively**: Setting deadlines can help to keep you accountable and focused, but make sure they are realistic and flexible enough to not cause unnecessary stress.

13. **Optimize Your Environment**: Create an environment that promotes efficiency. This could mean organizing your workspace, reducing distractions, or creating a comfortable home layout.

14. **Learn to Delegate**: Don't be afraid to ask for help or delegate tasks to others. This can free up your time for more important tasks or relaxation.

15. **Focus on One Thing at a Time**: Multitasking can be inefficient. Focusing on one task at a time can lead to better quality work and less stress.

16. **Use Your Leisure Time Wisely**: Choose leisure activities that relax and recharge you. This doesn't mean you have to be productive during your downtime, but rather choose activities that contribute to your overall well-being.

17. **Automate Finances**: Set up automatic bill payments, savings transfers, and investments. This habit takes the effort out of managing your finances.

18. **Cultivate Mindfulness**: Practicing mindfulness can help you stay focused on the present, reducing anxiety and stress. It's a simple way to bring quality to every moment.

19. **Seek Continuous Learning**: Be open to learning new ways to simplify and improve your life. This can mean reading books, attending workshops, or listening to podcasts.

20. **Celebrate Small Wins**: Recognize and celebrate your small achievements. This can boost your morale and motivate you to continue your efforts.

Small steps for major impacts

The journey through the realms of strategic laziness and the adoption of life-changing lazy habits leads us to an essential understanding: small steps can indeed create major impacts. This philosophy is not just about finding shortcuts or avoiding effort; it's about intelligent and conscious living where every small action is a part of a larger, more effective strategy.

The Ripple Effect of Small Changes

Each small habit or technique discussed in the previous chapters, while seemingly insignificant on its own, contributes to a larger pattern of behavior that dramatically shifts how we approach life and work. Just like a single pebble can create ripples across a vast body of water, a small change in routine or mindset can propagate through all aspects of our lives, leading to significant transformations.

Sustainability of Small Steps

One of the key reasons small steps lead to major impacts is their sustainability. It's often easier to integrate and maintain a small habit into your daily life than to attempt a large-scale, radical change. These small adjustments are less overwhelming and more adaptable to different life circumstances, making them more likely to stick in the long term.

Cumulative Effects Over Time

The true power of small steps lies in their cumulative effect. Just as compound interest grows wealth slowly but exponentially, small, consistent changes in behavior accumulate over time, leading to outcomes that far exceed the sum of their parts. This principle applies to productivity, personal development, relationships, and even health and wellness.

The Power of Incremental Improvement

The concept of 'kaizen,' or continuous improvement, emphasizes the value of making small, ongoing positive changes. By focusing on incremental improvement rather than immediate perfection, we set ourselves on a path of continual progress. Each small step forward builds upon the last, leading to substantial growth and development over time.

Embracing Flexibility and Adaptability

Small steps inherently allow for greater flexibility and adaptability. As we navigate the complexities of life, our circumstances and priorities can shift. Small, manageable adjustments can be more easily modified or redirected, ensuring that our approach to life and work remains relevant and effective.

In conclusion, 'The Art of Laziness' is not an ode to idleness, but a tribute to the wisdom of working smarter, not harder. It advocates for a life where small, lazy yet effective techniques and habits lead to significant and sustainable impacts.

CHAPTER 15
The Magic of 80/20

"Focus on the vital few, not the trivial many. The magic of the 80/20 principle is in realizing that less effort can lead to more joy and greater results."

- Richard Koch

Life often resembles a relentless race. We hustle, strive, and push, aiming to squeeze every drop of productivity from our days. Yet, amid this chaos, a simple, almost magical principle exists, offering a breath of fresh air. This principle is known as the 80/20 rule, or the Pareto Principle. It whispers a curious truth: 80% of our results come from merely 20% of our efforts.

Unearthing the 80/20 Rule

The 80/20 rule isn't new. It's been around since the early 1900s, discovered by Vilfredo Pareto, an Italian economist. Pareto noticed something peculiar about his garden peas: 20% of the pea pods held 80% of the peas. Intrigued, he applied this observation to wealth distribution in Italy and, astonishingly, found a similar pattern: 20% of the people owned 80% of the land.

This principle, however, isn't just about peas or wealth. It's a universal truth that applies to almost every aspect of life and work. Think about it:

- In a business, 20% of the customers often bring in 80% of the profits.

- In personal productivity, 20% of our tasks contribute to 80% of our success.

- In daily life, 20% of our possessions are used 80% of the time.

Embracing Laziness with 80/20

Now, let's talk about laziness, but not the kind you're used to. This laziness is strategic, smart, and surprisingly productive. It's about finding that golden 20% and focusing your energy there. Why? Because it's in this 20% that the magic happens.

Imagine cutting down your to-do list to just the tasks that really matter. Or focusing on the few clients who bring you the most joy and profit. That's not just simplifying work; it's amplifying results.

How to Apply the 80/20 Rule

1. **Analyze Everything**: Look at what you do, who you spend time with, and where you put your energy. Identify the 20% that brings the most positive results.

2. **Eliminate or Delegate**: Let go of or delegate the 80% that's less productive. It's not about doing more; it's about doing more of what works.

3. **Focus and Amplify**: Give your best to the crucial 20%. Nurture it, grow it, and watch as it transforms your work and life.

4. **Regularly Reassess**: What's your 20% today might not be your 20% tomorrow. Keep evaluating and adjusting.

Living the 80/20 Way

Living by the 80/20 rule is liberating. It's about being smart with your effort, not just hard work. It's about finding balance, reducing stress, and enjoying the journey. Remember, sometimes less is more, and in the case of the 80/20 rule, less effort can indeed lead to more success.

Now, let's dive into a deeper, more personal aspect of laziness - finding joy in doing less. It's not just about being productive; it's about being happy.

The Myth of Busyness

Our society often equates busyness with success. If you're not busy, you're not working hard enough, not ambitious enough. But is that really true? Being constantly busy can lead to burnout, stress, and a joyless existence. What if doing less could actually make us happier and more fulfilled?

Embracing Joyful Laziness

Joyful laziness is about finding delight in doing less. It's about savoring moments, indulging in rest, and choosing activities that bring genuine happiness. It's not about being idle; it's about being intentionally selective with how we spend our time.

How to Find Joy in Doing Less

1. **Prioritize Happiness**: Identify what truly makes you happy. Is it spending time with family, reading a book, or perhaps pursuing a hobby? Make these a priority.

2. **Learn to Say No**: You don't have to agree to every request or attend every event. It's okay to say no and reserve time for yourself.

3. **Simplify Your Life**: Declutter your schedule and your surroundings. Less clutter means more space for joy.

4. **Mindful Rest**: Resting is not laziness; it's necessary for rejuvenation. Be mindful about your rest periods. Whether it's a short nap, a walk, or just sitting quietly, let it be a time of recharge.

5. **Celebrate Small Joys**: Find joy in the little things - a cup of coffee, a sunny day, a good conversation. Happiness often hides in simple moments.

The Balance of Laziness and Productivity

Finding a balance between laziness and productivity is key. It's not about choosing one over the other but integrating both into our lives harmoniously. By applying the 80/20 rule and embracing joyful laziness, we can create a life that's not only successful but also deeply fulfilling and happy.

The art of laziness, when practiced wisely, can be a powerful tool. It's not about shirking responsibility or being unproductive. It's about being smart with our efforts and finding joy in simplicity. As we master the magic of 80/20 and the art of doing less, we open doors to a more balanced, joyful, and successful life.

CHAPTER 16
Parkinson's Law in Practice

"Parkinson's Law dictates that 'work expands to fill the time available for its completion.' This principle reminds us to work smarter, not harder. By setting clearer, tighter deadlines and focusing on efficiency, we can accomplish our tasks with greater effectiveness and less stress."

- Cyril Northcote Parkinson

We've all heard the saying, "Work fills the time available for its completion." This is Parkinson's Law, and it's not just a clever quip; it's a profound truth that shapes our lives. The idea is simple: the amount of work we have expands to fill the time we give it. But what does this really mean for us in our day-to-day lives? How can understanding and embracing this law change the way we approach our tasks, our time, and ultimately, our lives?

First, let's consider what Parkinson's Law does not mean. It doesn't suggest that we should rush through our tasks or do them poorly. Nor does it imply laziness in the traditional sense. Instead, it invites us to a deeper understanding of how we allocate our most precious resource: time.

The Elasticity of Time

Time is elastic in the sense that our perception of how long a task takes is often dictated more by the time we allot to it than by the task itself. Have you ever noticed how a two-hour task can mysteriously expand to fill an entire day? This isn't magic; it's Parkinson's Law in action.

To harness the power of this law, start by setting more defined limits. Give a task half the time you usually would. You'll be surprised how often you complete it in the allotted time without a significant drop in quality. This isn't about cutting corners; it's about cutting out the unnecessary and the unproductive.

Quality Over Quantity

A common misconception is that more time equals better work. But Parkinson's Law challenges this notion. By limiting the time we spend on tasks, we're forced to focus on what truly matters. This often leads to better, more efficient work. It's about achieving quality through limitation, not despite it.

The Hidden Benefits

Embracing Parkinson's Law has unexpected benefits. It can lead to increased creativity as you're forced to find more efficient solutions. It can improve decision-making, as you have less time to waffle over choices. It fosters a sense of urgency that can be incredibly motivating. And perhaps most importantly, it can lead to a better work-life balance, as you reclaim time that was once lost to the abyss of unproductive work.

Rethinking Effort

The mantra of working smarter, not harder, is about reevaluating our approach to work. It's not about avoiding hard work; it's about making sure that the hard work we do is effective. This means being strategic about how, when, and where we work.

Prioritize Wisely

Start by identifying the tasks that have the most significant impact. What are the 20% of your efforts that yield 80% of your results? Focus on these tasks. This is the essence of working smarter. It's not about doing less work; it's about doing the right work.

Leverage Tools and Techniques

In today's world, there's an abundance of tools and techniques designed to boost productivity. From time management apps to project management software, the right tools can make a massive difference in how efficiently we work. But remember, tools are only as effective as the person using them. Choose the ones that best fit your workflow and use them wisely.

Embrace Rest and Reflection

Working smarter also means recognizing the value of rest and reflection. Regular breaks aren't a sign of laziness; they're a vital component of sustained productivity. Use these moments to step back and reflect on your work. Are you on the right track? Is there a more efficient way to achieve your goals?

Cultivate Continuous Learning

Finally, embrace the mindset of continuous learning. The world is constantly changing, and so are the ways we work. Stay curious and open to new methods, ideas, and approaches. This doesn't mean chasing every new trend but being willing to adapt and grow.

The Art of Laziness isn't about being lazy in the traditional sense. It's about being smart with our time and our effort. By embracing Parkinson's Law and learning to work smarter, not harder, we can achieve more with less, find greater satisfaction in our work, and, most importantly, reclaim time for the things that truly matter in life.

CHAPTER 17
Japanese Secrets for Everyday Ease

"Do not fear going slowly; fear only standing still."

– *Chinese Proverb*

Laziness is often misunderstood. In the Western world, it's synonymous with idleness, a lack of ambition, a waste of daylight. But travel eastward to Japan, and you'll discover a perspective where laziness isn't just tolerated; it's an art, a philosophical stance, a secret ingredient to a life well-lived.

Embracing 'Nagomi': The Harmony of Being

In Japan, there's a concept known as 'nagomi'— harmony. It's not just a word; it's a lifestyle, a goal, a journey. Nagomi is about balance, about finding peace in your environment, and about letting that peace seep into your soul. This pursuit of balance often leads to practices that Westerners might label as laziness.

Take, for instance, the art of 'Niksen'—the Dutch concept of doing nothing, or more precisely, the art of doing something without any purpose. In Japan, this translates to moments of reflection, staring out a window, watching the rain, or simply sitting with a cup of tea, letting thoughts drift like leaves in a slow-moving stream.

The Power of 'Ma': Embracing the Space in Between

'Ma' is another Japanese concept pivotal to understanding their version of laziness. It refers to the space between things, the pause between actions, the silence between notes. In music, it's the rest; in art, the blank space; in life, the moments we often rush through or skip entirely.

In the West, time is money, efficiency is king, and productivity is the altar at which we worship. But in Japan, 'Ma' teaches us that the pauses are just as important as the actions. The space between tasks is not wasted; it's an opportunity for our minds to rest, our creativity to breathe, and our souls to find tranquility.

The Zen of Imperfection

Wabi-sabi, the acceptance of imperfection, is another cornerstone of the Japanese art of laziness. It's the appreciation of the beauty in the incomplete, the flawed, the impermanent. This philosophy liberates one from the relentless pursuit of perfection—a race that often leads to burnout and dissatisfaction.

In the context of laziness, wabi-sabi reminds us that it's okay not to be busy all the time. It's okay to have moments of unproductivity, to have hobbies that aren't monetized, to simply be without the need to justify our existence through constant output.

Ancient wisdom for modern laziness

Ancient wisdom from various cultures provides a rich tapestry of insights into the art of laziness. These philosophies, though centuries old, offer refreshing perspectives in our fast-paced, modern life.

The Greek Philosophy of Leisure: Schole

The ancient Greeks, particularly the philosopher Aristotle, had a concept called 'schole,' which translates to leisure. But their understanding of leisure was not idleness. It was the time spent away from work to engage in self-reflection, learning, and personal development.

In modern terms, 'schole' aligns with the idea that our value isn't tied solely to our work or productivity. Leisure time isn't just a break from work; it's an essential component of a well-rounded, fulfilling life. It's in these moments of 'laziness' that we often find our most profound insights and experience personal growth.

Siesta: The Wisdom of Rest

Siesta, a tradition in Spain and some other parts of the world, is a short nap taken in the early afternoon, often after the midday meal. This custom isn't just about avoiding the midday heat; it's about understanding the natural rhythms of the human body.

Modern science backs this up, showing that our circadian rhythms naturally dip in the early afternoon, making us less alert. The siesta is an ancient response to this, a form of laziness that is actually in tune with our biological needs, leading to improved productivity and well-being.

The Roman 'Otium': The Noble Art of Downtime

The Romans had the term 'otium', which referred to a time of leisure and rest, particularly enjoyed by the upper classes. It was a time for intellectual pursuits, for hobbies, for enjoying the arts, and for socializing.

In today's world, 'otium' can be a guiding principle for our downtime. It's not just about doing nothing; it's about engaging in activities that nourish our souls, that bring us joy and relaxation, and that ultimately make us more rounded, happier individuals.

In conclusion, the art of laziness is not about wasting time; it's about understanding the value of time. It's about recognizing that our worth is not solely defined by our productivity, and that rest, reflection, and leisure are not just essential for our wellbeing but are valuable in their own right. Whether it's through the Japanese 'nagomi', the Greek 'schole', or the Roman 'otium', each culture offers a unique perspective on how to master this art and live a more balanced, fulfilling life.

CHAPTER 18
Night Rituals for a Better Tomorrow

"Rest is not idleness, and to lie sometimes on the grass under trees on a summer's day, listening to the murmur of the water, or watching the clouds float across the sky, is by no means a waste of time."

- John Lubbock

Nightfall brings a gentle curtain over the day's hustles, an opportunity to recharge and prepare for what lies ahead. Embracing laziness, in this context, isn't about neglecting duties; it's about understanding the vital role of rest and relaxation in enhancing our productivity and overall well-being.

The Uncelebrated Virtue of Slowing Down

In a world that praises the busy and the productive, slowing down seems almost revolutionary. Yet, it's in these quiet moments of doing 'nothing' that we often find our greatest insights and rejuvenate our weary minds and bodies. Night rituals are not about doing more but about doing differently - engaging in activities that soothe rather than strain, that prepare us not just for the next day but for a more harmonious life.

Crafting a Personal Night Ritual

A night ritual need not be elaborate or time-consuming. It's about creating a space where you can unwind and reflect. Consider these simple steps:

1. **Digital Detox**: Begin by disconnecting from the digital world. Turn off your gadgets, or at least put them aside, an hour before bed. This disconnection from constant stimulation is a vital step in calming the mind.

2. **Creating a Sanctuary**: Make your nighttime space a sanctuary. This could mean tidying up, dimming the lights, or adding elements like scented candles or soft music that signal to your body that it's time to wind down.

3. **Reflective Journaling**: Spend a few minutes jotting down your thoughts, reflections, or even a list of things you're grateful for. This practice helps clear the mind and fosters a sense of contentment.

4. **Mindful Reading**: Rather than consuming content digitally, opt for a book. Reading can be a wonderful way to transport yourself into different worlds, easing the day's stresses.

5. **Gentle Movement**: Engaging in gentle, restorative physical activities like stretching or yoga can help release physical tension, preparing your body for a restful sleep.

The Science of Sleep and Rest

Science underscores the importance of quality sleep and relaxation. Sleep isn't just a period of inactivity; it's a crucial time for the body and brain to repair, regenerate, and reorganize. Poor sleep habits can lead to a host of health issues, from cognitive impairments to increased stress levels. By establishing night rituals, you're not just indulging in laziness; you're investing in your health.

End your day to start anew

Concluding your day effectively is akin to setting the stage for the morrow. It's about ending one chapter so the next can begin afresh, unburdened by the residues of yesterday.

The Art of Letting Go

One of the most important aspects of ending your day is the art of letting go. It involves releasing the day's worries and stresses, and understanding that holding onto them will not change the past but can certainly mar the future. Here's how you can practice this:

1. **Mental Release**: Engage in a mental exercise where you visualize the day's events and consciously release them. This could be through meditation or a simple mindful breathing exercise.

2. **Physical Unwinding**: Engage in activities that help your body relax. This could be a warm bath, a relaxing walk, or even some light stretching exercises.

3. **Setting Intentions for Tomorrow**: Spend a few minutes planning for the next day. This isn't about detailed scheduling but more about setting a general intention or goal. This practice gives a sense of closure to the current day and a direction for the next.

4. **Gratitude Practice**: End your day on a positive note by acknowledging the things you're grateful for. Gratitude shifts focus from what's lacking to what's abundant in our lives.

Embracing Rest as a Path to Renewal

The concept of laziness is often laden with negative connotations, yet in the art of ending your day and starting anew, what we term as 'laziness' is actually a form of self-care and renewal. It's about understanding that rest and relaxation are not just rewards but essential components of a balanced, productive life.

In essence, 'The Art of Laziness' is about redefining our relationship with rest and leisure. It's about recognizing that in the stillness and quiet, in the moments of 'doing nothing,' we find the strength and inspiration for all our 'doing.' As we embrace these night rituals and learn the art of ending our day, we set ourselves up not just for a more productive tomorrow, but for a more fulfilled, balanced, and joyful life.

CHAPTER 19
Tiny Habits, Huge Difference

"Do not underestimate the power of a small action; one step can start a journey of a thousand miles."

- Lao Tzu

In a world that seems to race at the speed of light, the notion of embracing laziness may sound counterintuitive, even rebellious. Yet, there lies an unspoken truth in the art of doing less: it is not about fostering idleness but about mastering the art of efficiency through tiny habits. This chapter is not a call to lethargy, but an invitation to a journey of meaningful minimalism in our actions.

The Magic of Micro Moves

Consider for a moment the humble ant. Observably industrious, yet each movement is measured, and purposeful. Humans too can learn from this. Small, well-thought-out actions can lead to significant changes. The concept is simple – start with a tiny habit, so minute that it almost feels too easy. The idea is to bypass the overwhelming feeling that often accompanies the thought of making a change.

Starting Small

The beginning of this journey can be as simple as waking up five minutes earlier or reading a page of a book each night. These tiny habits are deceptively powerful. Over time, these minutes add up, and the pages turn into chapters. The key here is consistency. A small habit consistently practiced becomes a powerful force over time.

The Ripple Effect

Imagine throwing a pebble into a still pond. The impact, though small, sends ripples across the entire surface. Similarly, tiny habits create ripples in our lives. Waking up five minutes earlier could lead to a small period of meditation or planning the day ahead. Reading a page nightly might ignite a love for literature or a thirst for knowledge. These ripples can extend further, influencing other aspects of our lives, leading to a cascade of positive change.

Embracing Efficiency

Efficiency is doing more with less, and this is where the art of laziness shines. By focusing on small, efficient actions, we eliminate the unnecessary, leaving room for what truly matters. This approach is not about cutting corners but about trimming the excess, streamlining our lives to focus on what's essential.

The 80/20 Rule

Consider the Pareto Principle, commonly known as the 80/20 rule. It states that approximately 80% of effects come from 20% of causes. Applied to life, this means that most of our results come from a small portion of our efforts. Identifying and focusing on these key efforts can lead to significant outcomes without the need for overwhelming exertion.

Laziness as a Tool

Here, laziness is redefined. It's a tool that teaches us to question the necessity of each action. Do we need to have a fully packed schedule, or can we achieve more with fewer but more significant tasks? This form of laziness is not about doing nothing – it's about doing what matters in the simplest, most effective way.

Building on the concept of tiny habits, this chapter delves into how these small changes can architect a substantial life transformation. The art of laziness here is about being smart with our efforts, ensuring each action has a purpose and contributes to a larger goal.

The Compound Effect

The compound effect is the principle of reaping huge rewards from a series of small, smart choices. What starts as a minor adjustment accumulates into significant life changes. It's like a snowball rolling down a hill, gathering more snow and momentum as it goes.

Consistency Over Intensity

The beauty of the compound effect lies in consistency. It's not the intensity of the action but the regularity that counts. For instance, exercising for ten minutes every day is more impactful than a two-hour workout once a month. Consistency turns these small actions into habits, and habits form the framework of our lives.

Patience is Key

In a world addicted to instant gratification, patience is a virtue that stands in stark contrast. The art of laziness encourages a patient, steady approach. Change might not be apparent immediately, but with time, the cumulative effect of these small changes becomes profound.

Simplifying for Significance

In simplifying our actions, we amplify their significance. By reducing the clutter of unnecessary tasks and distractions, we allow ourselves to focus on what truly adds value to our lives.

Decluttering the Mind and Space

Decluttering isn't just physical. It's also mental. Simplifying life involves clearing the mind of unnecessary worries and focusing on the present. This mental decluttering gives way to clarity and purpose in our actions.

Prioritizing What Matters

In the art of laziness, every action should be purposeful. Prioritizing means understanding what is truly important and letting go of what is not. It's about recognizing that not all tasks are created equal and focusing on the ones that have the most significant impact.

The Joy of Slowness

Lastly, this chapter celebrates slowness. In a fast-paced world, slowing down can be revolutionary. It's about enjoying the journey, not just racing towards the destination. Slowness allows us to savor experiences, deepen relationships, and appreciate the small, often overlooked aspects of life.

Mindfulness in Action

Practicing mindfulness is a way of embracing slowness. It's about being fully present in each moment, engaging with each task mindfully. This approach leads to a deeper understanding of ourselves and our surroundings, enriching our experiences.

Quality Over Quantity

In embracing the art of laziness, we choose quality over quantity in everything we do. This principle applies to work, relationships, experiences, and material possessions. It's about appreciating and making the most of what we have, rather than constantly seeking more.

In conclusion, this art, when practiced diligently, can transform the way we live, work, and interact with the world around us.

CHAPTER 20
Pomodoro: Short Sprints to Success

"Rest is not idleness, and to lie sometimes on the grass on a summer day listening to the murmur of water, or watching the clouds float across the sky, is hardly a waste of time."

— John Lubbock

In the bustling corridors of our daily lives, where the ticking clock is a relentless master, there exists a paradox. This paradox lies in the heart of what many would call laziness, but I prefer to term 'strategic restfulness'. It's an art, really – the art of knowing when to pause, when to breathe, and when to channel your energies in short, powerful bursts. This art, when practiced well, can transform the way we work, live, and achieve our goals. And at the heart of this transformation is a simple, yet revolutionary technique known as the Pomodoro Technique.

The concept is disarmingly simple: work in short, focused sprints, followed by brief periods of rest. The traditional structure is 25 minutes of concentrated effort, followed by a 5-minute break. These intervals are known as 'Pomodoros', named after the tomato-shaped kitchen timer that Francesco Cirillo, the inventor of this method, used during his university days.

The Power of Short Bursts

You might wonder, how can working less lead to more productivity? The answer lies in understanding our brain's capacity for focus. It's a well-known fact that the human mind can only concentrate effectively for a limited period. By breaking down work into manageable chunks, the Pomodoro Technique ensures that we operate at our peak capacity.

Furthermore, the enforced breaks serve as a reset button, not just for our brains but for our entire being. These pauses are not just about physical rest; they're an opportunity for mental and emotional rejuvenation. This cyclical rhythm of work and rest aligns with our natural energy fluctuations, making our work more sustainable and less exhausting.

Laziness or Efficiency?

At first glance, taking regular breaks might seem counterintuitive, especially in a culture that often equates busyness with productivity. However, this is where the beauty of 'strategic restfulness' comes into play. By being lazy - in a structured way - we're actually being more efficient. This technique transforms the guilt often associated with taking breaks into a productive tool.

The Pomodoro Technique isn't just about working smarter; it's about living smarter. It's a reminder that rest is not the enemy of productivity; rather, it's its ally. In embracing this, we learn the art of balancing effort with relaxation, of intertwining urgency with calmness.

Implementing Pomodoro in Your Life

Adopting the Pomodoro Technique in your life is straightforward. All you need is a timer and a task. Start by choosing a task you want to accomplish, set the timer for 25 minutes, and work on the task until the timer rings. Then take a short break, reset, and start again. After four Pomodoros, take a longer break.

As you integrate this technique into your routine, you will notice a change. Tasks that seemed daunting become manageable. Procrastination, often a byproduct of feeling overwhelmed, diminishes. Your work starts to align with your natural rhythm, leading to a more fulfilling and less stressful life.

The timer technique that transforms

In an era where multitasking is often glorified, and constant busyness is a badge of honor, the idea of using a timer to enforce periods of rest might seem archaic. Yet, it is this very simplicity that makes the timer technique a transformative tool in mastering the art of strategic laziness.

The Psychology of Time

Our relationship with time is complex. We often feel as though we are racing against it, trying to squeeze in as much as possible. However, when we break time down into manageable segments, something magical happens. Our brain's perception of time shifts. We no longer see a daunting, endless stretch of work but rather a series of manageable intervals.

The timer brings a sense of urgency and focus. Knowing that the clock is ticking, we become more efficient and more driven. It creates a healthy pressure that propels us to concentrate and reduces the temptation to give in to distractions.

The Restorative Power of Breaks

The breaks in the Pomodoro Technique are as crucial as the work intervals. These breaks serve multiple purposes. They are not just a time to step back from work but also a moment for self-reflection, relaxation, and mental clarity. This is where the concept of laziness is redefined. It's not about doing nothing; it's about doing what is necessary for our minds and bodies to recover and function optimally.

During these breaks, step away from your work environment. Stretch, take a walk, meditate, or engage in a non-work-related activity. This detachment is vital. It allows you to return to your task with a fresh perspective and renewed energy.

Practical Tips for Implementing the Timer Technique

1. **Choose the Right Timer**: It can be a physical timer, a phone app, or computer software. The key is to have a distinct signal that marks the end of a work session and the beginning of a break.

2. **Create a Conducive Environment**: Minimize distractions during your Pomodoros. Inform those around you of your schedule to avoid interruptions.

3. **Be Strict with Time**: Adhere to the timings diligently. Resist the urge to skip breaks or extend work sessions.

4. **Reflect and Adjust**: Use the breaks to assess your work. What have you achieved? What needs more attention? Adjust your plan accordingly.

5. **Enjoy Your Breaks**: Embrace the art of doing nothing. Let your mind wander, daydream, or engage in a relaxing activity. This mental relaxation is key to the technique's success.

The art of laziness, as portrayed through the Pomodoro Technique and the timer method, is not about shirking responsibilities or work. It's about understanding and respecting our natural rhythms, harnessing our peak periods of focus, and allowing ourselves the time to recharge. In doing so, we become more productive, more creative, and ultimately, more fulfilled.

Embrace the timer, respect your need for rest, and watch as the art of strategic laziness transforms your work and your life.

CHAPTER 21
5 Minutes to Motivation

"Laziness is nothing more than the habit of resting before you get tired."

– Jules Renard

It might come as a surprise that sometimes, the secret ingredient to success is a touch of laziness. Yes, you read that right. Laziness, often misunderstood as the enemy of productivity, can actually be its ally. This chapter is not about encouraging idleness, but rather about understanding how strategic laziness can lead to an explosion of motivation and productivity when used wisely.

Laziness is typically seen as a lack of effort or a reluctance to work. However, what if we reframe this notion? Consider laziness as a natural response of your body and mind seeking rest and rejuvenation. It's a signal, not a flaw. Acknowledging this can be the first step in harnessing its power.

The Role of Rest
Rest is not just a pause between periods of work; it's an integral part of the creative and productive process. It allows your mind to wander, which can lead to

innovative ideas and solutions that wouldn't emerge in the midst of non-stop activity. Embracing moments of laziness can, paradoxically, be a path to higher productivity.

5-Minute Motivation Boosters

1. **Micro-Meditation**: Spend five minutes in quiet reflection or meditation. This brief pause can reset your mind, providing clarity and renewed focus.

2. **The Power of Daydreaming**: Allow yourself a five-minute daydream. Letting your mind roam freely can spark creativity and unexpected bursts of motivation.

3. **Nature Break**: Step outside for five minutes. The change of scenery and fresh air can invigorate your senses and refresh your perspective.

4. **Quick Physical Activity**: Engage in a short burst of physical activity, like stretching or a brisk walk. This can energize your body and mind.

5. **Write It Down**: Spend five minutes writing down what you're feeling or what's blocking you.

Sometimes, acknowledging these feelings on paper can diminish their power over you.

The key is to listen to your body and mind. When they ask for a break, give it to them. But remember, the goal is not to indulge in laziness indefinitely. It's about using these moments strategically to recharge and then move forward with greater energy and motivation.

While laziness can be a hidden ally, there are times when we need to kickstart ourselves into action quickly. This chapter explores simple, yet effective techniques to transform the energy of laziness into immediate, productive action.

Breaking the Inertia

The hardest part of any task is often starting it. Overcoming this initial inertia is crucial. Here's how:

1. **The Five-Minute Rule:** Commit to doing the task for just five minutes. Often, starting is all it takes to continue.

2. **Break It Down:** Divide your task into smaller, manageable parts. Tackling these smaller pieces feels less daunting and helps build momentum.

3. **Change Your Environment:** Sometimes a change in surroundings can stimulate action. Move to a different room or workspace to shift your mindset.

4. **Visualize Success:** Spend a minute visualizing the completed task. Seeing the end result in your mind can be a powerful motivator.

5. **Accountability Partner:** Tell someone about your goal. Knowing that someone else is aware of your task can push you to get started.

Embracing Imperfection

Perfectionism can be a form of procrastination. Accept that not everything has to be perfect. Sometimes, good enough is just fine, especially to get the ball rolling. Allow yourself the freedom to make mistakes; it's often through these mistakes that we find the most growth and learning.

Reward Yourself

Plan a small reward for completing the task. It could be something as simple as a cup of your favorite coffee or a short break. This gives you something immediate to look forward to and serves as motivation to get moving.

The Role of Routine

Establishing a routine can help automate action. When something becomes a habit, it requires less mental effort to initiate. Start with small, daily routines and build from there.

The art of laziness is not about promoting idleness but about understanding and using our natural rhythms of rest and activity to our advantage. By embracing strategic laziness, we can find bursts of motivation and turn them into productive action. Remember, it's about working smarter, not harder, and recognizing that sometimes, a little laziness can go a long way.

CHAPTER 22
Consistency Made Simple

"Consistency is simplicity, and in simplicity there is elegance. Keeping up doesn't have to be a burden; it's about finding the right rhythm in the small, daily steps. This way, we grow without feeling weighed down."

- James Clear

We often hear that consistency is the key to success. But how do you remain consistent without succumbing to the overwhelming pressure of continuous effort? The answer lies in the art of embracing laziness strategically.

The Simple Philosophy of Doing Less More Often

The core principle here is not to overburden yourself. It's about finding the minimum effective dose of your activity. Consider a gardener who waters the plants just enough to keep them thriving, not so much that they drown. Your tasks, much like these plants, need regular, small doses of your attention.

1. Set Achievable Goals

Start with setting small, achievable goals. The satisfaction of completing a task, however small, is a powerful motivator. It's like cleaning a small section of a messy room. Once you start and see a clear area, you're motivated to clean a bit more.

2. The Power of Routine

Incorporate your tasks into a routine. A set routine reduces the mental energy required to start a task. Just like brushing your teeth is a non-negotiable part of your morning, let your small tasks be non-negotiable parts of your day.

3. Embrace Laziness

This might sound counterintuitive, but embrace your lazy moments. Sometimes, doing nothing is exactly what you need. It can be a moment of rest, a quick recharge before you go back to your small tasks. Remember, a bow too tightly strung will snap.

Keeping Up Without Feeling Down

Life is not a race, but more like a stroll through a park. Keeping up with responsibilities doesn't mean you have to be on a constant run. It's about walking at your pace, enjoying the scenery, and reaching your destination without feeling down.

The Art of Selective Participation

You don't have to jump on every opportunity or participate in every activity. Be selective. It's okay to say no. Prioritize tasks and activities that align with your values and goals. This selective participation ensures you don't spread yourself too thin.

1. Quality Over Quantity

Focus on the quality of your work rather than the quantity. It's better to have a few well-done tasks than a myriad of half-baked projects. Quality work is satisfying and less draining in the long run.

2. Find Joy in Little Things

It's essential to find joy in the small, everyday things. Whether it's a cup of coffee, a walk in the park, or a good book, these moments of joy can recharge you and give you the strength to keep up with your tasks.

3. Stay Connected

Maintain a support system. Talk to friends, family, or colleagues. Sometimes, just talking about what's on your plate can lighten the load. They might offer perspectives or solutions that you hadn't considered.

The art of laziness is not about shirking responsibility; it's about smartly managing your energy and time. It's about understanding that rest and relaxation are not the antithesis of productivity but are essential components of it. By embracing this art, you can remain consistent without feeling overwhelmed and keep up without feeling down. Remember, it's the balance of activity and rest that leads to sustained productivity and happiness.

CONCLUSION
Embrace Your Laziness

"Embrace your laziness, for it is in stillness that the most profound thoughts arise. Let your mind wander in the quiet moments, for there, you will find wisdom and insight."

- Alan Watts

Laziness often gets a bad rap. It's labeled as the enemy of productivity, the antithesis of ambition, and the root of all procrastination. But what if I told you that laziness when understood and harnessed correctly, can be a hidden treasure in our fast-paced world?

The Power of Strategic Laziness

Laziness isn't just about lounging on the couch all day. It's a state of mind that encourages us to seek the path of least resistance. And this isn't always a bad thing. Think about it – the greatest inventions were born from the desire to make tasks easier and less time-consuming. Laziness can be a powerful motivator for innovation and efficiency.

Listening to the Lazy Mind

Our lazy moments can be our most creative. When we're relaxed and not actively engaging in complex tasks, our minds wander. This mental wandering is a key ingredient for creative thinking. It's when we come up with our best ideas – the kind of ideas that seem to spring out of nowhere.

The Art of Delegation and Automation

Laziness teaches us the importance of delegation and automation. Why spend hours on a task that can be efficiently handled by someone else or by an automated system? Learning to delegate and automate doesn't just free up your time; it also empowers others and leads to more productive and creative systems.

Rest as a Productivity Tool

In our relentless pursuit of productivity, we often forget the importance of rest. But rest is crucial for rejuvenation and maintaining long-term productivity. The art of laziness includes recognizing when your body and mind need a break. It's about understanding that sometimes, doing nothing is the most productive thing you can do.

The Lazy Path to Success

Success and laziness are not mutually exclusive. By embracing the art of laziness, we can find more efficient, creative, and enjoyable paths to our goals.

Prioritizing What Truly Matters

Laziness forces us to prioritize. When you're inclined to do less, you naturally focus on the tasks that offer the most significant benefits. This means cutting out the fluff – those tasks that take up time but don't contribute much to your goals.

The Joy of Slow Living

There's a growing movement around the world that embraces slow living – a lifestyle that emphasizes a slower approach to aspects of everyday life. This approach aligns closely with the art of laziness. It's about savoring the moment, appreciating the small things, and not rushing through life.

Embracing Imperfection

The pursuit of perfection can be exhausting. Laziness teaches us to embrace imperfection. Not every task needs to be completed to a flawless standard. Sometimes, 'good enough' is enough. This mindset can significantly reduce stress and increase happiness.

The Lazy Millionaire

Even in the business world, there's room for laziness. Many successful entrepreneurs have mastered the art of working smarter, not harder. They build systems that run themselves, create passive income streams, and focus their efforts only on what truly matters – the quintessence of laziness.

Embrace Your Laziness

As we wrap up our journey through the art of laziness, it's important to remember that laziness is not about shirking responsibility or ambition. It's about finding smarter, more enjoyable ways to achieve our goals. It's about listening to our bodies and minds, and not being afraid to take the path of least resistance when it makes sense.

So, dear reader, as you turn the last page of this exploration, remember that your lazy moments might just be your most productive. Embrace your laziness, for it might lead you to a life of greater efficiency, creativity, and joy. After all, the path to success doesn't always have to be the hardest one – sometimes, the lazy way is the best.

9 781963 674040